Press

I0141055

Nathaniel Brimmer-Beller

methuen | drama

LONDON • NEW YORK • OXFORD • NEW DELHI • SYDNEY

METHUEN DRAMA
Bloomsbury Publishing Plc, 50 Bedford Square, London, WC1B 3DP, UK
Bloomsbury Publishing Inc, 1359 Broadway, New York, NY 10018, USA
Bloomsbury Publishing Ireland, 29 Earlsfort Terrace, Dublin 2,
D02 AY28, Ireland

BLOOMSBURY, METHUEN DRAMA and the Methuen
Drama logo are trademarks of Bloomsbury Publishing Plc.

First published in Great Britain 2025

Photography by Yussef Soudan

A catalogue record for this book is available from the British Library.

Library of Congress Control Number: 2025938732

ISBN: PB: 978-1-3505-8210-1
ePDF: 978-1-3505-8211-8
eBook: 978-1-3505-8212-5

Series: Modern Plays

Typeset by Mark Heslington Ltd, Scarborough, North Yorkshire

For product safety related questions contact
productsafety@bloomsbury.com.

To find out more about our authors and books visit
www.bloomsbury.com and sign up for our newsletters.

PRESS

written by

Nathaniel Brimmer-Beller

Also by Nathaniel Brimmer-Beller

Plays
Mack The Knife
Technicolor
Chagos 1971
Oklahoma June '74
Fear of Roses
Blood Red Apples and Deep Gold Honey
The Kindness of Strangers
In Everglade Studio
Nines
And I Mean That Sincerely
The Net Under Makeout Bridge
Port City Signature
The Spare Room

Films
Happy Birthday
I Love You
The Gips Incident
Four Jews
Evening Plans
The Arbitrator
B-Roll

Radio
Turner & Turner

Monologues
The Mission of Harper's Ferry
The Nomineers

For my friend Emily

Who never skipped a smile
Brought a good time everywhere
A friend 'til the end, a fountain of fun
She knew it's what a maverick would've done
She was that sort of bear

Words can't express everything
I think laughing does the rest
You showed me that
The greatest gift

– NBB

Thanks to

Avery, my love

to Mom, Dad, Grandma, Tawny, Sandy

to Rosie, Sophie, Yussef, Niamh, Phoebe, Esalan

to Nic, Sian, Callan, to Methuen Drama

to all the actors, technicians, staff,
and enthusiastic theatre people who have
helped my plays come to life over the years

~~Smack Wave~~ Black Bat
wouldn't be here without you

Nathaniel Brimmer-Beller | David Fring, Writer, Director

Nathaniel Brimmer-Beller is a playwright, actor and director originally from Washington, DC, now living in London. He has directed more than thirty theatrical productions, and has written more than twenty plays, including six acclaimed premieres at the Edinburgh Festival Fringe and three plays published worldwide.

His play *In Everglade Studio* enjoyed a month-long run at the Edinburgh Festival Fringe in 2023, where the play was longlisted for the BBC Writersroom Popcorn Award for Best New Writing. *In Everglade Studio* transferred to The Hope Theatre in April 2024, where it ran for an acclaimed three-week engagement and was the first of Brimmer-Beller's plays to be published by Methuen Drama.

His next play, *Port City Signature*, selected to re-open The Hope Theatre as the first major production of its new era, also had an acclaimed three-week run in 2024. This seaside noir thriller became Brimmer-Beller's second play published by Methuen Drama, and featured original song 'port city', written and sung by avery.

Brimmer-Beller's play *Blood Red Apples and Deep Gold Honey* was nominated for the George Devine Award for Most Promising Playwright in 2022. This philosophical comedy-drama explored his mixed-race and Jewish heritage, and was developed through the Almeida Theatre's Anthem project.

Brimmer-Beller's Edinburgh Festival Fringe plays have transferred to London on multiple occasions – most notably his lauded, darkly comedic, political satire *Chagos 1971* in 2019, and his fast-paced Hollywood awards-industry satire *Press*, in which Nathaniel has portrayed the play's lead character, David Fring, since its premiere. In 2023, he developed David's personality into a monologue performance and television concept titled *The Nomineers*, which earned him a Bursary Prize at the writer-performer competition Screenshot, organised by South of the River Pictures and SISTER Global. After the competition, panel judge Olivia Colman called Nathaniel 'a f**king great actor'. This he will not soon forget.

Other recent theatrical works written by Nathaniel include 1960s-fashion-world mystery *Nines* and satire of the contemporary theatre industry *The Kindness of Strangers*, both of which enjoyed successful runs at the Canal Cafe Theatre. *The Kindness of Strangers*, originally developed as a double-bill with *Press*, transferred to VAULT Festival in 2023.

Nathaniel wrote, directed and edited the short film *Evening Plans* in 2021, which was nominated for Best Short Film in the New Visions category at the Edinburgh International Film Festival. He also wrote the radio play *Turner & Turner*, and the acclaimed Edinburgh Festival Fringe plays *Mack The Knife, Technicolor* and *Fear of Roses*. He wrote, directed and edited the short film *B-Roll* in summer 2024, which premiered in London at Side/Step Festival in 2025.

Nathaniel studied International Relations at the University of Edinburgh, and received an MA with Distinction in Film Studies from King's College London.

Nathaniel is also a professional screen actor, as well as experienced film editor, audio producer, graphic designer, screenwriter, film scholar and horse rider. He continues to write plays, films, prose and more.

brimmerbeller.com

Rosie Hart | Kate Smalls

Three days before the debut of *Press* at the Edinburgh Festival Fringe (2021) both actors were pinged for Covid and had to isolate. Rosie Hart stepped in, learning the two-hander in seventy-two hours. She performed with Nathaniel Brimmer-Beller, collecting a few 5-star reviews along the way!

Rosie Hart is a writer and actor hailing from the Highlands of Scotland. Rosie trained at the Royal Conservatoire of Scotland, during which she received the Pauline Knowles Scholarship for most promising female actor, the Norah Cooper Mulligan Award for working with verse, the Duncan Macrae Competition Prize for best performance in Scots language and the Charles Brooke Memorial Prize for work in Scots verse.

Theatre credits include: Trace in *Nines* with Black Bat Productions, Evelyn in *Takin' Over the Asylum* with the Royal Conservatoire of Scotland, Colleague/Jo in *Parliament Square* with the Royal Conservatoire of Scotland, Kate in *Press* with Black Bat Productions, Lady Macbeth in *Macbeth* with the Royal Conservatoire of Scotland.

Screen credits include: Jay in *Dog Squad* (CBeebies), Katie in *Dead Weight* (NFTS), Olive in *Other People With Beautiful Names*, Callie in *Bookmarks*.

Rosie is a published poet whose work has been featured in exhibitions/publications across Europe, including *Weaving Bodies* 2023 (The Hidden Gardens) and Stellar Quines' 2021 project *How to Change the World*.

Niamh Jones | Producer

Niamh Jones is a Welsh producer and writer. She has just begun her producing journey, having produced several student productions, but has been a part of the theatre world for as long as she can remember.

Having spent most of her childhood acting, Niamh transitioned into crew roles during her time at university. She worked as a marketing manager on numerous shows, most notably holding the role for the Oxford Student Opera Society for the academic year of 2023–4. Her directorial debut was Alan Bennett's *The History Boys* at The O'Reilly Theatre in 2023, where she sold out multiple nights. Following this, she held a role on the Oxford University Drama Society committee for 2023–4 and went on to direct the sell-out run of A. A. Milne's *Toad of Toad Hall* at The Michael Pilch Studio in 2023.

Niamh's first producing role was for Uğur Özcan's *The Sun King* during its run at the Edinburgh Festival Fringe in 2024. The semi-autobiographical coming-of-age fantasy premiered earlier the same year with Jones' production company, Peedie Productions, with Jones acting as associate director on the project.

More recently, Niamh produced a short run of Christopher Hampton's *Les Liaisons Dangereuses* at the Oxford Playhouse in November 2024. This production utilised live cinema techniques and premiered a score written by Lou Newton. She also co-produced Oxford Student Opera Society's 2025 performance of Gianni Schicchi at Oxford Town Hall.

As a student Niamh began the theatre-reviewing blog Wild Rose and Pearls, where she regularly reviewed both student productions and professional works, becoming the most notable student reviewer in the city. Following graduation she has continued this blog and also works as a reviewer for *Broadway World*.

Niamh studied English Language and Literature at the University of Oxford.

Niamh is also a podcast host for *Noo's Nook*, where she reviews books, films and plays.

About Black Bat Productions

Black Bat Productions has been bringing curious audiences sharp, stylish and memorable pieces of theatre since its founding in 2017. The company strives to create work that can thrill, surprise, entertain and start conversations on the themes and perspectives at hand. What's a good play without a good think afterwards?

In addition to multiple London runs, Black Bat Productions has staged original work at the Edinburgh Festival Fringe seven times. Notable productions include the premiere runs of *Press* ('Genius . . . pleasurably wicked' – Monica Yell, *Broadway Baby*; 'Fringe theatre does not get much better than this' – Violet Mackintosh, *The Violet Curtain*), of *Chagos 1971* ('The most intelligent piece of theatre I have seen at the Fringe' – Annabel Jackson, *EdFringe Review*), and of *In Everglade Studio* ('an intelligently constructed masterpiece' – Jemima Hawkins, *The Student*).

In recommending *Fear of Roses* in 2021, All Edinburgh Theatre wrote of Black Bat Productions: 'Anyone who has seen one of their previous productions will recognise several of the elements on display . . . a noirish sheen, taut and snappy dialogue, a clever script with well-engineered twists, an almost miraculous cool.' In recommending *In Everglade Studio* in 2023, calling it 'Nathaniel Brimmer-Beller's most impressive piece to date,' All Edinburgh Theatre wrote: 'As was the case with previous Black Bat productions, there is both a polished surface . . . and a profound undercurrent.'

In Everglade Studio was longlisted for the BBC Writersroom Popcorn Award for Best New Writing, transferred to The Hope Theatre in 2024 ('brilliantly written' – *The British*

Blacklist, 'genuinely breathtaking' – *The New Current*), and was published alongside the run by Methuen Drama. The British Blacklist listed *In Everglade Studio* among the Best Theatre of 2024.

Noir thriller *Port City Signature* was published by Methuen Drama later the same year, and selected to re-open The Hope Theatre in September 2024 ('a timeless, tense and tenacious tale' – *Broadway World*, 'a brilliant homage to Hitchcock and the film noir genre' – *RatedReviewed*). *Port City Signature* was nominated for an OFFIE for the production's set design.

Black Bat Productions continues to make work, for stage and for screen, in London and elsewhere.

blackbat.uk

Author's Note

Just after the end of the first-ever run of *Press*, I wrote the following about this play:

> Most plays I've written and/or directed are at least somewhat borrowing from something else – 40s noir movies, 60s sci-fi yarns, 70s political satire, 50s dime store literature, J-P Melville, Jim Thompson, Iannucci (big time), etc. But this particular hate-it-because-we-love-it focus on movies and what they mean/do to us in *Press* is the most honest and Me story I've put out there in my life, and it's been a serious honor feeling such a hearty, kind response in return.

I don't know how many thoughts I expressed in 2021 I would stand by today, but I stand by that.

Two months earlier, Black Bat Productions had a lot on its plate. We were putting together my three-hander all-female bank-robbery play *Fear of Roses* with the ever-gracious Assembly team, for a month-long Edinburgh Fringe Festival run premiering the first week of August. Then one day in July, the also lovely Pleasance team get in touch. There's an opportunity to fill a scheduling gap in their beautiful Cabaret Bar.

I tell them as *Fear of Roses* is nicely set up and settled at the Assembly Roxy, we'd likely have capacity for a second production. But what? The other Fringe-length shows I had already done, or had written and ready to do, required too many actors and moving parts to put together just then. So I ask them: What if I write something new? Just for this. They say send something and let's see. Now I have a play to write, that goes up in two fortnights.

I wrack my brain for the better part of an afternoon. I happened to be in France at the time. I take a thinking-walk along the Cote d'Azur – one of those places so profoundly beautiful it tends to remind one life is very much worth living after all, come what may. But I had a project to imagine up, so paradise went largely ignored, while I did some thinking.

I open Notes app, and thank stars I'd kept it at least somewhat organized over the years. There's a folder in there called Ideas, and I parse through it for plausible two-, *maybe* three-hander projects. I find a note from 14 June 2016, which says this:

> play: *Press*
>
> The final day of the publicity circuit, with the Oscar nomination announcement looming, of a divisive Civil War film that cast a white man in a role meant for a former slave.

I turned right around, and once I'd sat down at a makeshift desk where I was staying, I wrote the first three-quarters of *Press* in one sitting.

The play premiered 17 August 2021, and played twelve performances to entirely sold-out audiences. The show was attended by some real Hollywood names, who, according to the staff of the theatre, were laughing quite heartily, particularly at the script's most twisted jokes, so make of that what you will.

Press has been performed twice with Pleasance in Edinburgh, twice at The Old Red Lion in Islington, put on elsewhere in London, at play-reading groups, for invited private audiences, for one-off live-streamed performances, and by a certain stretch of the imagination, at the Royal Court – when David Fring was reinvented into monologue piece and TV story *The Nomineers,* for writer-performer event Screenshot.

In the years since *Press* premiered, I've had an amusing amount of friends and acquaintances share headlines and rumours with me all about the real-life entertainment industry imitating nails-down-chalkboard jokes in this play: big-ticket nomination scandals, awards campaign scheming and trickery, head-spinning casting decisions, ingeniously sneaky backroom deals to avoid public scrutiny, you name it. What a world. Like I wrote back then, any hate you may pick up on for What The Movies Have Become in *Press* is only masking a great deal of love and appreciation that anyone is still interested in movies at all. Let that good work never cease, silly as it gets. Silly and *stupid* as it sometimes gets.

I didn't write *Press* so I could play David. Far from it – originally, David and Kate were both white. Three days before we opened, two isolation-mandating pings meant we suddenly had no cast for our two-hander play. The show must go on, so we reasoned I'd step in as David, at least for the first performance. Thanks in no small part to the exceptional Rosie Hart learning Kate at lightning speed – gamely reflecting our real-life whirlwind problem-solving onstage – we were all happy to find that first performance went well.

The team and some friends in the audience had a thinking-chat later that day, and agreed that watching David played this way had worked for them, more than expected. There was something thornier, stranger, more brash, more exciting about watching this fairly uncommon juxtaposition of message and messenger. Non-white actors were not expected to play this type of character. We weren't meant to be saying these kinds of things, about these kinds of topics. To this day it still jars some people. Surely we're meant to be playing characters with an unassailable moral clarity, or, failing that, the requisite contextual justification for their faults and a clearly communicated path to redemption. The noble victim. The noble revenger. The noble scion of the community. Leave the moral grey areas to the white actors and white characters. They can handle them.

Yawn. I could go on about these ubiquitous, insidious invitations to shun our own individuality; the vilification of critical thought, particularly when such thought or individuality might risk our membership to a self-stereotyped tribe; how often our self-worth is sold back to us as a brazenly anti-intellectual oversimplification of ourselves, of life's unanswerable questions, of the joys of being an unclassifiable individual.

But I'll arrive at the point. Playing David with that then-problematic juxtaposition was much more fun than the 'right' way ever could be. It still is. I hope that's true for anyone who plays the part.

It's one of the greatest joys of my creative life to laugh at the world together with open-minded people. *Press* has been an addictively fun way to do that. To this day I'm glad that note survived five years in the cloud until the moment I needed it.

I am very happy and grateful to share what became of that idea with you.

I hope you enjoy *Press*, and thank you, as always, for reading something I've written.

Love,
NBB

Photograph taken by Niamh Jones. Pictured: Rosie Hart, Nathaniel
Brimmer-Beller. 2025.

EMANCIPATION, n. A bondman's change from the tyranny of another to the despotism of himself.

> He was a slave: at word he went and came;
> His iron collar cut him to the bone.
> Then Liberty erased his owner's name,
> Tightened the rivets and inscribed his own.

– Ambrose Bierce, *The Devil's Dictionary*

Press

Characters
David Fring
Kate Smalls

Time
Modern day.

Place
1. The TV studio of *Entertainment Now*.
2. The Smack Wave Office.

Notes
BlackBerrys can be used as David and Kate's phones. We found there's something anachronistically funny about that. Who knows why.

Excerpts of Joe George Frampton's *Catch Me Some Freedom* experience are available, should you wish to experience them. These include Mama Gertrude's speech, and one of Chase Witley's most moving scenes as Charlie Joe Shimley.

Rules
The only rule is that David and Kate are from different countries.

The only other rule is have fun.

1

Entertainment Now

Audience-in music fades.

Chipper morning news tunes fade in. A soft studio light dimly shines on **David Fring***, ready for his interview.*

Nicely dressed in a three-piece suit, eager to charm. Perfect morning show guest.

Whenever his attention drifts, **David** *finds a speck of dust to clear from his lapels, or he peers around the studio.*

Entertainment Now (*voiceover*)
And welcome back, it's *Entertainment Now*, you're here for all things glitz, glam and glorious and it's a very special day for the movies. The Goldie nominations are upon us in only a few short hours. And to talk about his high hopes for his newest venture, we are with David Fring –

Just when he's paying attention least, intensely bright lights illuminate **David***.*

He blinks but keeps a gigantic smile on his face.

Entertainment Now (*v/o*)
– one of the producers of the sure-to-be-acclaimed and by all accounts ascendant new film *Catch Me Some Freedom*, the brainchild of wunderkind filmmaker Joe George Frampton, whose previous work *My Dead Uncle's Bones* was notoriously snubbed for a Best Picture nom by the Goldies three years ago. But now Frampton is back, early buzz seems to be positive, particularly given the authentic, diverse and *timely* nature of the film's story and subject matter, and you, David, are waiting on good news. How do you feel?

David
Hello! Hello. Thrilled, everyone at Smack Wave Films is honored and thrilled that *Catch Me* is being talked about as

a big thing in the wings. Fingers crossed for an excellent
Goldies announcement morning!

Entertainment Now (*v/o*)

In the wings is right, David, now *Catch Me Some Freedom* is
a special case for the Goldies, yes? As it has yet to screen
for almost any public audience, you have embargoed
critics' reviews of the film until today, and only opened
screenings to a handful of members' groups, which in sum
total, some have noted, includes the entire Goldie
selection committee.

David

Yes, but that's all a matter of industry jargon, really. I
wouldn't want to bore your viewers with complicated
details like that.

Entertainment Now (*v/o*)

Of course. Let's just say you're following an
'unconventional' release schedule before opening up to
the wider public, or indeed any public at all, is that right?

David

Yes, that's right. We felt the story's message was best
r-released all at once. Joe George is such a powerful artist,
and storyteller, and we felt the point of the piece, and the
subject matter, was best understood without any . . .
interference, before the people got a chance to embrace it.
We also – I'll give you a quick peek behind the curtain,
actually – we do, like you say, have high hopes for the film,
and if the Goldie Committee agrees with us that this
important, timely, authentic . . . lly diverse work is exactly
the kind of important conversation and subject matter we
should be discussing right now, and the nominations do
flow in, we hope that will help boost the film's release later
this week, so it can really reach the audiences it needs to
reach, and start the important conversations, that we
should be having, right now.

Entertainment Now (*v/o*)
Yes, important conversations indeed. This is a big film for a company like Smack Wave, we hear, possibly a make-or-break moment for you.

David
It, well, it could be, we, hope –

Entertainment Now (*v/o*)
Some call your company an underdog. Some call you an upstart. Some might even say you –

David
As long as we're not an updog!

Entertainment Now (*v/o*)
What is upd–

Silence. **David** *smiles toothily.*

The voice exhales. **David** *squirms.*

David
S-sorry, I –

Entertainment Now (*v/o*)
Tell us a little about the company, David.

David
Well, we . . . I, I founded Smack Wave Films as a, to, because – to tell stories. Stories that storytellers want to tell and stories that story-listeners want to have had told to them by storytellers who value substance and style, but above all, story. And, this – this story is one of true, unique *blistering* authenticity, because it really happened, and what could be more authentically . . . than that?

Entertainment Now (*v/o*)
Authentic indeed. You and Smack Wave are poised, David, to pull off what could be a head-turning rags-to-riches, obscurity-to-relevance tale here, with *Catch Me Some Freedom* topping prediction lists in many Goldie categories, many more so than only a few weeks ago, when

few people had heard of the film, or indeed your company or indeed, you. How have you pulled this off?

David

Oh, trade secrets now – a lady never tells.

Entertainment Now (*v/o*)

Well, how about you tell us.

David

Ooh, you're trying to loosen my lips on Live TV, huh?

Entertainment Now (*v/o*)

Excuse me?

David

Sorry, no, I, well, we, myself and my colleague Kate we, we took a look at the industry as it is and as it has become to be, and we, well, during and after this look we came up with a system we think breaks it down quite nicely. PLAP.

Entertainment Now (*v/o*)

Sorry?

David

PLAP.

Entertainment Now (*v/o*)

'PLAP.'

David

Yep. It's our little shorthand, for how we make sure our well-oiled marketing machine is oiling up the body and soul, the innards and the outards of every Goldie voter there is as much as it possibly can. Let me explain. Standing a fighting chance of getting any nomination boils down to four distinct categories, we like to say: Prestige, Likeability, Appeal, and Performance.

Prestige. That speaks for itself. It's gotta be nice, nice to look at, nice to think about. Gotta be glam, as you put it. The old razzle dazzle. Larger than life. Prestigious! Even slaves can put a little concealer on, smooth up the edges, you know? Um.

So, and then Likeability. That speaks for itself, really. No one would have voted for Hitler! Well, I guess, they did, but . . . you wouldn't do it now. Why? Because he's not likeable.

Let's see. Appeal. You've got to have appeal. Appeal is really about . . . being likeable, I guess.

And finally, Performance. How does it do, in the wild? And that's what we're going to find out when the film opens, when *Catch Me Some Freedom* opens, when Joe George Frampton's *Catch Me Some F* –

Entertainment Now (*v/o*)
Joe George adapted it from a story he heard on his travels in the American South, is that correct?

David
Yes, that's correct. Joe was backpacking, on a wilderness retreat. It's something he likes to do. He's such an elemental artist –

Entertainment Now (*v/o*)
Yes, like he is right now we understand.

David
That's –

Entertainment Now (*v/o*)
On a retreat.

David
Yes, that's right –

Entertainment Now (*v/o*)
Because otherwise we would have had *him* here.

David
R-right, yes. So. So Joe George was in Mississippi, a site of *so* much pain . . . and, well, he loves to speak to locals

wherever he goes, and while he was there, he met some people, some really intriguing, inspiring, intriguing people. And they told him this story. A story of such inspiring, human resilience, and almost superhuman strength, and . . . humanity. And he knew, he had to tell that story. He had to get that story heard by . . . people. So that became *Catch Me Some Freedom*, and we are so glad, that it did.

Entertainment Now (*v/o*)
Of course. The story revolves around a group of enslaved people who escape a plantation under cover of night, yes?

David
Yes, that's right.

Entertainment Now (*v/o*)
So they escape the Carruthers Plantation, this is of course at the height of slavery in America.

David
Such a painful thing.

Entertainment Now (*v/o*)
And they find themselves on the doorstep of –

David
Charlie Joe Shimley, yes. A white man, a former overseer at the plantation in fact, who for the first time in his life takes mercy on the poor devils, and who grows to understand, love, and even act as something of a father figure to these runaway . . . enslaved people. In many ways, we like to say, he catches *himself* just as much freedom, as the s-sl-slav- . . . as they do. So there's something for everyone.

Entertainment Now (*v/o*)
And Shimley is played by Chase Witley, star of the runaway success reality series *Hot Bods*.

David

Yes. We were so happy to get Chase, and I think Joe
George has brought out a side of him that audiences will
not have seen before. Although I suppose they've already
seen quite a lot of him on *Hot Bods*!

Entertainment Now (*v/o*)

And Mr Witley, a white man, plays the lead.

David

Yes, that's . . . that's right.

Entertainment Now (*v/o*)

I wonder if you could comment, David, on reports that
surfaced recently, as recently as this morning, in fact, that
this story, a true one in most ways –

David

Yes. Yes, a true one. Joe George is so focused, on telling,
important, true stories, like this one, with honesty and
bravery, and –

Entertainment Now (*v/o*)

By all accounts, the character of Shimley was a real
person, Charles Shipman, who had worked on the
plantation in the past and knew the escaped personally.

David

Right. Yes. It's such a powerful story, and . . . the
timeliness of it . . . and, what we love about what Chase
brings to the role is this ineffable, almost boyish –

Entertainment Now (*v/o*)

But historians have now pointed out that Charles Shipman
was an African-American. A former enslaved person
himself.

David *has no idea what to say.*

A very long pause.

David*'s eyes are frozen, so unblinking his corneas start to burn a
little.*

David

. . . Yes.

Entertainment Now (*v/o*)

Did you not know that previously?

David

No, we – we did. He, well, that's, that history is, that aspect, of it, is, uh, we understand, to some, in some degree, of dispute –

Entertainment Now (*v/o*)

Dispute?

David

Not dispute, no, uh . . . Joe is such a powerful s-storyteller . . .

Entertainment Now (*v/o*)

Right.

David

Such a free spirit . . . in-in front of, uh, b-behind the camera, behind the story, behind important stories, like this one –

Entertainment Now (*v/o*)

So you *were* aware that your film changes the race of who is essentially the protagonist, from a Black person to a white one.

A long pause.

David

Joe feels . . . such a deep . . . connection, to the . . . Black experience.

Entertainment Now (*v/o*)

How is that?

Another long pause.

David *blinks.*

David

W-well! Well! His great-grandfather was, was a West Indian day-laborer, not slave-uh, sl-slaved, not one of them. At all. He was free as a bird. Free, free to go and make Joe George's grandfather exist, and what a gift that was. To us, and . . . and to cinema. And t-to these, uh, im-im-important, uh, c-c-conversations –

Entertainment Now (*v/o*)

David Fring. Smack Wave Films. The movie is *Catch Me Some Freedom*. We will see shortly what the Goldies, and the public, have to say about it. David, thank you.

David

Th-thank – thank *you*, for – Oh.

David *stammers out the beginning of a response but the lights black out.*

2

The Smack Wave Office

Lights up. A sparse office.

Kate Smalls *sits still but is quite panicked.*

One hand scrolls through social media on her phone, the other quickly leafs through an old book, looking more and more pained as she gets through both of them.

Kate
. . . Ohh, that's not good. That's not goood. That one's creative. But not good.

David *rushes in, a vision of barely-collected stress.*

David
Answer a question, Kate.

Kate
Sure.

David
Two questions.

Kate
Sure thing.

David
Maybe more.

Kate
As many questions as you want, David.

David
One. First question.

Kate
Right.

David
How bad is it?

Kate

Okay, well –

David

Two. Second question.

Kate

Are we –

David

Yes, let me get it all out. Answer at the end.

Kate

Right.

David

The second question is, are we in trouble?

Kate

Mmhm.

David

'Mmhm' as in yes, or 'mmhm' as in you register the question?!

Kate

Well, both, honestly.

David

Answer at the end!

Kate

Right, sorry.

David

Third question. If we are in trouble, how much trouble? Similar to the first question I admit.

Kate

I agree.

David

Fourth question. *Is this bullshit?*

Kate

Well . . .

David

Fifth and final question, for now.

Kate

For now.

David

Can we make Joe take the blame for it?

Kate

Joe as in Joe George?

David

Joe as in Joe George.

Kate

Right.

David

Got that?

Kate

I do.

David

Okay. Answer time.

Kate *counts backwards on her fingers.*

Kate

In random order. No, Joe George is completely off the grid and he will be for a week.

David

Completely?

Kate

Middle of absolute nowhere. No chance.

David

Great.

Kate (*next finger*)
We are in trouble.

David
Great.

Kate (*next finger*)
Probably a lot.

David
Cool.

Kate (*next finger*)
It's very bad. The feeds could not be more upset. Little digital pitchforks all around.

David
And the final question.

Kate
It depends. Should people hate us for this? I don't know. Probably not. Do some of them have something of a point . . .

David
No. No! They do not.

Kate
Have you read what they're saying?

David
No, but, I bet it's . . . shit.

Kate
Right. Well it's all from this book –

David
Of course! Some flavour-of-the-week pop-theory hokum, right?

Kate
It's this historical account, of the whole Shipman thing. It won a bunch of academic awards, there's a quote from someone I'm pretty sure is pretty famous on the back.

David

Well did you Google what it says?

Kate

Well I found it.

He notices the book.

David

Oh.

Kate

And I've been reading it.

David

How did you find it?!

Kate

It was in the library.

David

They had that in the library?!

Kate

Yes, it's a book.

David

Where? The Oxford book vault?!

Kate

The cute one down the street. It's great.

David

So it says what about Shimley – Witley –

Kate

Shipman.

David

Yes. What, you agree with them now?!

Kate

Well I've been reading it and . . .

David

And what?! How bad is it for us?

Kate

It's, uh . . . it's, yeah it's pretty bad.

David

Shit.

Kate

For us I mean. The book is actually really well written.

David

Why is it bad?!

Kate

The guy's *definitely* Black.

David

Which guy?

Kate

Shipman. Shimley. The guy who we made white. Or Joe George did, and we, uh, backed up with a few million dollars.

David

Fuck. Are they sure?! Are there photos?

Kate

From the nineteenth century?

David

When did they do photos?

Kate

After that. There is a sketch though.

David

Let me see.

He grabs the book.

He sees the sketch.

He winces.

Kate

He's *definitely* not Chase Witley.

David

No he is not. Shit.

Kate

So.

David

So.

Kate

What . . . do we do now?

David

You're asking me?!

Kate

Like you always like to say, David, you've been at this game longer than me.

David

Yes but Kate this is your territory, surely you know how to deal with whatever this is turning into. I'm taking a back seat. I already shat the bed on *Entertainment Now*.

Kate

You weren't that bad. You looked nice.

David

I did? You didn't see me sweating through my shirt?

Kate

. . . Nnope.

David

And besides, when they asked me about Shimley I made such an *ass* out of myself, I'm afraid some daytime-television-watching morons may have looked past the pretty colours and listened to what I actually . . . said.

Kate

A rare happening, but you may be right.

David

And if *Twitter's* gotten involved . . .

Kate

It has.

David

Then you need to get busy fixing it, Kate! You speak that language. You need to convince them, somehow, that making some old Black guy white really isn't that bad. That can't be that hard! There's no way we could have known this would have been an issue. Sue me, but I don't keep up with current affairs and that type of thing.

Kate

It's not really current, it happened 200 years ago.

David

Well no one's given a shit about Charles Shipman since then, either! I can tell you that much. No one even knew he was Black!

Kate

I think some Black people might have.

David

. . . Oh you're wrong this *is* bullshit.

Kate

I said it depends!

David

Isn't it!

Kate

Well . . .

David

It is!

Kate

It's true that, I mean, he's . . . not meant to be white.

David

So what if he's white?! Lots of people are white! You're white! My postman's white. You don't see that many of them. So.

Kate

Yeah but Shipman wasn't.

David

Well –

Kate *gestures to the phone.*

Kate

And plenty of these people ripping the piss out of us aren't either.

David

That surprises you?

Kate

Usually in these matters it's the eager-beaver white kids who try to get out in front and complain louder than everybody else, but currently it's neck-and-neck. We must have really gotten to them.

David

So what is this rainbow coalition saying?

Kate

They're saying, well, what you'd expect.

David

What?

Kate

Basically that we should have gotten someone, well, Black. Or at least Blacker than Chase Witley.

David

I've had glasses of milk Blacker than Chase Witley. Oh, what were we supposed to do?! I've been in this business a long time, Kate. Do you know how hard it is to find Black talent?

Kate

I have an idea.

David

So you understand!

Kate

It's not very hard at all.

David

Chase is a perfectly nice guy. They should not be taking this out on him. This is the problem, with –

Kate

They're not talking about him.

David

Oh, well then –

Kate

They're mainly talking about us.

David

Shit.

Kate

We've lost almost . . . eight thousand followers –

David

In a day?!

Kate

In an hour.

David

An hour.

Kate
They're throwing around a boycott.

David
Of the film?!

Kate
Of all our films.

David
Oh for fuck's sake let me see.

He takes her phone and stares at the screen.

David
Fuck me.

Kate
Yep.

David
God they hate us.

Kate
They do.

David
That one's creative.

Kate
It is.

David
They hate us so much! All we did was cast a guy who *happens* to be white. That's it! That's his only crime! It's not like he MeToo-ed anyone. That we know of . . . right?

She thinks.

He thinks.

Kate
Yeah . . . uh . . .

They both think, harder.

Kate

. . . yeah.

David

Yeah.

They nod, fairly sure.

David

. . . I almost wish he had, at least the press release for that is already written up and ready to go.

Kate

We do need a press release for this, though. Quickly, I'd say.

David

Would you. Why?

Kate

What do you mean why?

David

Can't we just let this blow over? These children will tire themselves out and move on to the next villain-of-the-hour any minute now.

Kate

David.

David

Kate?

Kate

What's today?

David

Oh fuck, the fucking *Goldies*.

Kate

Yeah.

David

When are they announced?!

Kate (*checks her watch*)
   Ffffff –

David
   Kate!

Kate
   About half an hour from now.

David
   Oh god.

Kate
   Yeah. And the trades say . . .

David
   What?!

Kate
   . . . we're in a very good position to . . .

David
   To what?

Kate
   . . . lead the nominations.

David
   . . . Is that bad, now?

Kate
   Think about it, David. You're right, people usually would
   get bored with this –

David
   Good, so?!

Kate
   But not if the Goldie Committee decides *Catch Me Some
   Freedom* is . . . By the way, I've never said this out loud to
   you, David, but that is just a *terrible* fucking title.

David

Oh, Kate, believe me, I know. But Joe George loved it
and honestly I assumed no one would ever watch it, but
apparently people 'care now' so just our fucking luck.
Go on.

Kate

If the committee decides it's one of the best films of the
year . . . It won't go away any time soon. Smack Wave will
have a giant fucking target on the middle of our collective
forehead for *months*, David. And if it *wins* anything!

David

It'll be *Green Book* on steroids.

Kate

Exactly.

David

God DAMMIT. Why did I let you talk me into an awards
push, Kate?!

Kate

Because I assumed it was a sure thing!

David

It is! That's the problem! You orchestrated an ingenious
campaign, flawless execution, an inordinate but successful
marketing budget. We PLAPped it as hard as we could.
But we PLAPped too well, Kate. And now if any of that
works, we're *fucked!*

Kate

Listen, we can handle this.

David

How?

Kate

What can be done, can also be undone . . .

David

Was that on your fortune cookie last night?

Kate

Yes, actually, it was. But in this case the cookie has a point.
I spearheaded this campaign, I can un-spearhead it. I can
headspear it.

David

In thirty minutes.

Kate

In thirty minutes. Or less.

David

Tell me who to call.

Kate *pulls out a notepad, searches through her contacts, and writes
down some names and numbers.*

Kate

Okay, we start with the big guns. Picture and Actor.

David

Picture and Actor . . .

Kate

Yeah.

David

This piece of shit is in the running for Best Picture of the
Year . . .

Kate

It is.

David

And Chase fucking Witley is on the verge of being a
Goldie-nominated performer . . .

Kate

It's a stupid business, David. But I ran a *class* campaign.
Inspirational. Messianic shit.

David

Well now we've got to take that wine, turn it back into
water, and piss it into the breeze.

Kate

Everyone knows Frank Waverly has a humongous sway in these things so let's start there. I got close with his daughter to get him to back the film's prospects. I'll call her first. Hold on.

Kate *sits back and calls, tapping her fingers.*

David *takes out his phone and writes some emails.*

When she gets an answer, **Kate** *beams and speaks in an entirely new tone of voice.*

Kate (*to the phone*)

Sarah! Hi! Hello! How are you?! It's Katie Smalls! Cupcake Katie! That's me. Yep. From – yeah, right you remember. Clever girl. Oh, that's great! That's so great, that's lovely. I bet it does. The one with – yes, oh that's great! Yes I'd *love* one but I'm at work, Sarah. Next time. Of course I'll wait, no problem!

She waits for a few moments.

David *notices how she's talking.*

David

Kate?

Kate

Yes?

David

How old is Sarah Waverly?

Kate (*to* **David***, rushed*)

Eleven.

Kate (*to the phone, immediately*)

Hellooo! Yes, yes how wonderful. Now Sarah I have a very important question, is Grampy Frankie there? Oh, oh alright, that's great, can you ask Grampy Frankie to call me when he's back? Soon, please Sarah? Amazing, you're so great. Enjoy the pool party!

She bluntly hangs up.

Kate

– *or whatever the fuck it was.*

David

What was that?

Kate

The business.

David

I've been in this –

Kate

Yes, yes, I know. Well if you want a win you have to get creative. And getting creative in this business is all about relationships, with a capital R. I think that's just as fundamental as Appeal and Performance if you ask me, but I did not like the sound of 'PLARP'.

David

No, me neither.

Kate

She's asking her grampy . . . grandfather to call me back.

David

Do we have time for that? Can't you just talk to him now?

Kate

He's taking a shit.

David

So, what, you can stalk pre-teen children but you won't speak to a grown man on a toilet?

Kate

Honestly, yes. Right, next, Len Vance, for the actors.

David

Oh I know Len, let me talk to him. He owes me an ice cream sandwich.

David *dials Len's number.*

Kate
  Why?!

David (*extremely innocently*)
  . . . Because I bought him an ice cream sandwich.

David *notices Len's answered his call.*

David (*to the phone*)
  Len! Lenny. David. Fring. Smack Wave . . . Yes. Right. Oh,
  oh you saw that. Yes, well . . . yes we're all very happy for
  Chase. He's . . . well that's what I wanted to discuss. We had
  a question, regarding later today, and . . . We . . . Well, we,
  uh . . . Would you give me a moment, Len? Just one minute?

He covers the phone.

David
  What the fuck am I supposed to say?!

Kate
  You asked to talk to him!

David
  Yeah well I wasn't fucking thinking ahead, was I. Tell me!

Kate
  Tell you what?!

David
  *How do I make Len make them not vote for White-Bread
  Witley?!*

Kate
  Honestly, I'd say tell them the truth.

David
  . . . Which one?

Kate
  That he can't act for shit.

David
Of course he can't act for shit, everybody already knows that,
Katherine. He's The Blonde One From Hot Bods.

David *hears Len talking and puts the phone back to his ear.*

David (*to the phone*)
Len! So sorry about that. We were just wondering how our
chances are looking, as per the Goldies . . . We need to
check up in light of . . . yes. Well, about Chase. He's, uh,
his involvement has taken on something of a new
dimension, and we . . . right. Yes, that's exactly what we
were thinking. Yes . . . The performances as a whole, or
. . . *his* performance? You liked that?

He covers the phone again.

David
They liked his performance. They thought it was great.

Kate
That is why you don't let actors vote for other actors.

David
What do I say?!

Kate
I don't know, tell him it's all been done before. You know?
It's derivative. I mean the amount of movies exactly like
this is just endless!

David
Kate!

Kate
Just try that.

David
Are you serious?

Kate
Yes! There's –

David
Telling them it's been done before will only encourage them!

He thrusts the phone back to his ear.

David (*to the phone*)
Len . . . Len?

He checks the screen.

David
Shit, he hung up.

Kate
Okay next is –

David
But I'm telling you, that strategy will not work.

Kate
Why not? He's just doing a rehash of Broderick in *Glory*, Brad Pitt in *12 Years*, McConaughey in *Free State of Jones* . . . McConaughey in *Amistad*, McConaughey in *White Boy Rick* . . . McConaughey in *Dallas Buyers Club* . . . McConaughey in *A Time to Kill* . . . McConaughey in *The Lincoln Lawyer* . . . boy, what does that say about Matthew McConaughey?

David
Broderick is great in *Glory!*

Kate
David have you seen *Glory*?

David
I, well, n-no, no one's seen *Glory*. But I've heard people say . . .

Kate
On to the next call.

David
Kate can we really do this?

Kate

What?

David

Save our asses in twenty minutes? They must have printed out the lists to read and everything already.

Kate

They can print new ones. It's a minute-to-minute business, David. If they smell enough shit radiating from *Catch Me Some Freedom*, some other Goldie bait will get the glory – we just need to clear the path.

David

But we can't convince and/or beg every voter who has sway on the committee in one morning.

Kate

No, just the ones who actually run it. Like Max Stamp.

David

You have Max Stamp's number?

Kate

I do.

David

Did you forcibly child-mind for him too?

Kate

Not quite. But I took a similar approach.

David

Not through the grandchildren?

Kate *dials the number.*

Kate (*to* **David**)
No, the grandmother.

Kate (*to the phone*)
Irene?! Good morning! Yes, I know! It's Katherine! Katherine Smalls. How are your petunias? Oh me I'm fine . . .

David (*simultaneously, unravelling*)
This is insane. This is insane! Why does any of this even matter?! It's happened before and people get over it! Kate! *Kate!!*

Kate (*simultaneously, to the phone*)
And how is Maxy? Is he busy right now? Could you, yes . . . yes, yes Irene if he could call me shortly, please? Wonderful. One second.

She covers the phone.

Kate (*to* **David**)
What is it?!

David
We're going to all this trouble to undo what should be a great success!

Kate *hangs up.*

Kate
They'll bury us, David! It'll be a big black mark – or a big white mark in this case – against us for the foreseeable. You'll have to either rename Smack Wave or . . . which, I've also never said out loud to you, but –

David
What?

Kate
Don't worry about it.

David
– But *is* it such a big deal, Kate? These things have happened, and people don't give a crap! No one said anything about DiCaprio, in *Blood Diamond*. No one said anything about Bullock, in *The Blind Side*. No one said anything about Stone, in *The Help*, and they fucking *worship* Atticus Finch! Are you gonna turn your back on Atticus *Finch?!*

Kate

Right but plenty of people *did* give a crap, to be fair, they just weren't, y'know, listened to at all.

David

Yeah, but real people. Normal people. They don't care!

Kate *puts her phone down and gestures at it.*

Kate

Well they do now! And if Chase Witley joins that list we'll never live it down. We'll either be laughing stocks or town pariahs, and that phone will stop ringing!

Her phone rings.

Kate

Hello? Frank! Frank, Frank, where to begin.

David

Well, I think we should fight it.

Kate (*to* **David**)

What?

Kate (*to the phone*)

Frank, one minute.

Kate (*to* **David**)

David, what?

David

Take a stand. I don't want to be pushed around by fourteen-year-olds on Twitter.

Kate

X.

David

Bless you.

Kate

R-right but, the fact still remains –

Kate (*to the phone*)
  – yes, yes Frank, right, I'm listening.

In a huff, **David** *gets out a stack of papers and sorts through them.*

Kate (*to the phone*)
  Right. Yes, we would appreciate it. Thank you, thanks a lot.

Kate *ends the call.*

David *finds what he was looking for.*

David
  There.

Kate
  Frank says if there's anything we can do about Picture, it's got to be a press release, but it can't come directly from us.

David
  Why not?!

Kate
  What do you mean 'there'?

David
  Why can't it come from us?

Kate
  He said it has to have an 'artist's touch'. If the company says something it'll seem like we're just worried about business.

David
  Who in their right mind would think that we aren't?

Kate
  The average consumer, David. What do you mean 'there'?

David
  I found this.

He holds up some paper.

David

From the script.

Kate

Of?

David

The shit-eating, *almost* heavily-nominated 'Joe George Frampton experience' *Catch Me Some Freedom*.

Kate

Oh, great. Why?

David

Needed to find the Goldie-Winning Monologue. Written exclusively for the purposes of winning a Movie Person a prestigious award. Here we go.

Kate

David, we really need to –

David

Now, what does it really matter what race anyone is, Kate? Hm? I'm gonna read this, as if I was, uh, white . . . and you're gonna pretend that I'm white, and you're gonna tell me if it's any less . . . timely! Any less . . . powerful! Or, diverse . . .

Note: If the actor's white, change it accordingly. Just make it the ravings of an unhinged chap.

Kate

Wait wait wait, is the character who's supposed to be Black more powerful if he's white? Is that what you're –

David

No! No . . . No, okay, I hear that now. No, okay, my point is better illustrated if . . .

He flicks through the script.

David

. . . Okay, here! Mama Gertrude, played by Delia, uh –

Kate
  Lewis.

David
  Delia . . .

Kate
  Lewis.

David
  Lewis! Right. Black in real life, Black in the movie . . .
  Wait, shit, is she getting nominated?

Kate
  Probably not.

David
  Okay, great.

He repositions.

David
  So, her big monologue goes like . . . and I want you to
  imagine me, like, *really* Black . . .

Kate
  David.

David
  So . . .

Kate
  David, I . . .

*He breathes in. Starts to realign his body to (how he thinks he
should) play the part. Should excruciatingly imply a pretty horrible
moment coming up.*

Kate *braces.*

David *opens his mouth to talk . . .*

David
  . . . I actually don't remember what point I was trying to
  make there.

Kate

Probably best we drop that line of argument.

He throws the paper.

David

Uhggghh, *fuck*. You're right.

Kate

I am. Now there's no need for us to fight right now, David. Between you and me we'll make it just in time, I'm sure of it.

David

Oh to do *what*, Kate? This is a lost cause!

Kate

Look, if we can work with Frank, he can get the film taken off the nomination list, once and for all, alright? He all but assured me.

David

Really?!

Kate

. . . I'm going to assume that's what he meant.

David

That's an awful lot of assuming, Kate! I mean I trust Frank Waverly more than most on these things, but *seriously* – I mean you just got through convincing me if both our names end up on that list, we can kiss Smack Wave farewell forever. Reputationally speaking.

Kate

Yes, I know, I'm good at that. Can we focus on this press release?

David

You trust him that much?

Kate (*already typing*)

Yes! I do. Now David –

David

What's his email?

Kate

What?

David

His email?

Kate

Frank@frank.com. He got in early on the whole email thing. Why?

David

Just curious.

Kate

David can we *focus on this press release!*

David (*typing the email into his phone*)

. . . Yes, yes. I thought it couldn't come from us?

Kate

We can't be the ones who say it, but we can be the ones who *write* it . . . you see.

David

Right.

Kate

Yes.

David

Let's do that.

Kate *takes out her phone.*

Kate

Open Notes app . . .

David

Joe George is definitely not around?

Kate

Definitely. He's in some country with little English and probably even less internet. Anyway, he wouldn't do it, and even if he did it'd be self-important horse-crap about artistic intention.

David

Well, if they're nominating his film maybe that's exactly what they want to hear.

Kate

That's . . . not a bad point.

David

How are you starting it?

Kate

I'll pull up our Apology Template first.

David's *phone rings. He answers it.*

Kate *types the press release while periodically checking on* **David**'s *tactics.*

David (*to the phone*)

Len! Len. Hello again . . . David. Fring . . . Smack Wave. Yes! Yes. Sorry about before. Yes, let's talk. Listen, Len, we – well, look at it this way, Len. We've had a bit of a change of heart, ourselves . . . Chase is great, but, uh, haven't the . . . Black people been through enough? Without the former star of *Hot Bods* mansplaining slavery to them? No, I do believe that. Listen, Len, as for Chase, he's wonderful, but his performance, it's . . . amateurish, derivative. He's basically just rehashing Broderick, in *Glory*, McConaughey in *Amistad* . . . And I love both those films! Loved. Loved, Len. Because I've Taken The Time. To listen, to learn, to do some . . . learning. And I don't like *Amistad* anymore! Yeah. There! I said it. Sue me, I don't like *Amistad*. And that was Spielberg so who the fuck is Joe George Frampton, you see what I'm saying? . . . Right, precisely!

Yes, no, exactly. I'm, I'm glad you agree. Okay, great, th-thank you, Len. Thank you so much.

He hangs up.

David

He said he'll see what he can do . . . What *can* he do?

Kate

I thought you'd been in this business a long time.

David

I've never had to *un*-campaign, excuse me.

Kate

Think about it like anything people vote on, David. A free and fair process, unless certain interests decide the freely and fairly chosen option isn't a very good one. In this case, if whatever friends we have at the Goldies decide to help, *Catch Me Some* fucking *Freedom* is out on its arse. Come see what I wrote.

David *takes her phone and reads the screen.*

David

Oh that's good. That's *good*. That sounds exactly like him. Oh god, yeah he would –

The phone rings in his hand. **David** *jumps.*

He hands it to **Kate***.*

David

Max Stamp!

Kate

I know!

Kate *answers the phone.*

Kate (*to the phone*)

Max! Yes, oh it sounds like she's doing very well!

David *checks his watch.*

David (*loudly whispering*)
  Let's speed this up.

Kate *nods.*

Kate (*to the phone*)
  Max, Max, I – right. I see. Right, okay. Yes, I understand,
  I'll get right on that. Yes, well me too. Okay.

She hangs up.

David
  What?

Kate
  He makes a good point.

David
  Okay, what?

Kate
  Now *he's* been in the business a long time.

David
  Okay, yes –

Kate
  A real *veteran*, I mean –

David
  What, Kate?!

Kate
  He said we need a swap. A sacrificial lamb. Something
  they can replace *Catch Me* with. You see?

David
  Okay . . . okay! That makes sense. We can do that. Easy.
  We can do that!

Kate
  What else is out this year?

David
  Fucked if I know.

Kate
 I'll check IMDb.

There's finally a pause.

David *thinks.*

Kate *scrolls.*

David
 You know, I was at that screening Joe had at his house the other day . . . Sorry, what does he call it, his *space* . . . and honestly, it wasn't even that good.

Kate
 Mmhm.

David
 I mean I know when people hear 'Civil War' and 'timely', whatever that means, they go bananas, but . . . you'd think someone would have stopped and said, this just *sucks*.

Kate
 Yeah.

David
 . . . What did you think of it?

Kate
 Hm?

David
 What did you think of *Catch Me*?

Kate
 Oh I don't really watch films. Here we go.

Kate *shows* **David** *the phone.*

Kate
 One of these prediction creeps has compiled real-time betting odds for each of the Prestige Picks for later today. You'll be happy to note . . .

She points to the screen.

David

Catch Me Some Freedom, coming in at number five . . .

Kate

They only nominate five.

David

But we're *at* five.

Kate

Right, but that's good. Six is only slightly lower odds, with seven and eight not much farther behind. We just need to get one of those movies into Frank and Len's lists, and Joe is history!

David

Great! Okay, let's see, what are they . . . sixth, *Adam's Apple*. What is that?

Kate

The new old-timey lesbian one.

David

Another?

Kate

Yep, another. This year it's *Adam's Apple* I guess. They got Diana Trenton and Hailey Robson doing the nasty this time, playing two sexually adventurous cavewomen who get stuck in a cave on a really stormy night in the Paleolithic era –

David

Alright, alright, I'll just watch that when I get home. Should we back that then?

Kate

Mm, it's all getting a bit samey, even for the Goldies. Keep reading, we can do better.

David

Okay, let's see . . . number seven, *The Mariner*. Oh, that's the Brent Harken one!

Kate

Yeah, the old trying-to-make-an-action-star-a-serious-
actor ploy. And trying it on with Brent Harken, I mean –

David

I love Brent Harken.

Kate

Of course you do.

David

He's *going* to win Best Actor for it, everyone knows that.

Kate

But the film's not up for any main awards other than that,
is it?

David *checks.*

David

. . . No.

Kate

So what does that tell you?

David

It's shit?

Kate

Exactly.

David

Yeah that probably does mean it's shit.

Kate

We ask 'em to pick *that* as Best Picture they'd laugh at us.
Even more than they are already.

David

Good point.

Kate *checks her watch.*

Kate
They've really got to just eat this one right up like a hungry sow at slop hour, David. Next. We can do this.

David
Okay! Yes, okay, alright . . . Eighth most likely: *Avalanche Canyon*.

Kate
I don't know that one?

David
Okay. Let's see . . .

David *gasps*.

David
Oh, yes.

Kate
Yeah?

David
Oh Kate it's perfect.

Kate
Go on!

David
Skimming the synopsis . . . it's a book adaptation . . .

Kate
Okay, great start . . .

David
Oh Kate.

Kate
Go on!

David
About a dead parent . . .

Kate
Yes . . .

David

No wait . . .

Kate

Oh no?

David

Dying parent!

Kate

Oh yes!!! That's so good, go on . . .

David

Mental health concerns!

Kate

Great.

David

Grappling with the welfare state!

Kate

Excellent!

David

They're *poor!*

Kate

I love it!

David

And the main character . . . is *struggling with his sexuality!!*

Kate

No!!

David

Yes!!

Kate

Oh thank the sweet tiny baby Lord Jesus for all he gives!

David

I think we've got it!

Kate
We're saved!

David
That's our sacramental lamb!

Kate
R-right! Yeah!

David
So now what?

Kate
I'll call Max.

David
Guess I'll call Len! What are we saying?

Kate
One thing and one thing only: our mistake boys, *Artichoke Canyon* is the film of the year!

David
Brilliant. Forget our dumb campaign! It's *Avalanche Canvas* over Joe George's piece-of-shit slavery thing!

Kate
Perfect!

She speaks into the phone.

David *psychs himself up for his own call.*

He gets an email, reads it intently.

Kate (*to the phone*)
Max! Max . . . Max.

Kate's *face changes.*

Kate (*to the phone*)
Max, one second, give me one second, will you? One minute.

Kate *lowers her phone.*

David

What is it?

Kate

David, what are we . . . We're literally about to campaign for our competitors.

David

Yes.

Kate

Against ourselves.

David

Under *extreme* duress!

Kate

But David, isn't –

David

Kate the announcement is minutes away, we have to –

Kate

But couldn't there be something . . . *something* . . .

David

What?!

Kate

The film, that Joe's made. That, let's not forget, *we* made.

David

We, well – okay, yeah?

Kate

I just remembered Joe coming in here, still buzzing from the reception *Dead Uncle's Bones* got at festivals. I remember him pitching it to you, you seemed genuinely moved.

David

Well . . . I feel passionately that slavery was bad.

Kate

Right, me too.

David

And it's very important to me that other people know, that I think that.

Kate

Right, exactly, me too.

David

So what's your point?

Kate

Well . . . I just can't quite stomach, throwing all of this, everything the film can be, away.

David (*checking his watch*)
All of a fucking sudden, Kate!

Kate

– just sinking our own ship like this . . .

David *checks his phone, begins writing an email as he says the following.*

David

The ship is a problematic ship! It, and we, would be dead in the water.

Kate

I mean doesn't the *story,* the *subject*, still have something . . . that can be, at least a little bit . . .

David

What?

Kate

Profitable?

David *pauses.*

He lowers his phone for a moment.

David

. . . Go on.

Kate

Well, think about it. Yes, initially, the reaction will be bad. Right now I'd guess, not *too* bad. I'd wager if it gets any nominations it'll be in something most people don't give two shits about, like Sound, or Writing. But even so, if enough people notice this movie did what it did, yes, Twitter might get out the pitchforks and try to eat our ass for breakfast.

David

That didn't sound quite right . . .

Kate

But imagine, David, if . . . instead of the Must-See, Must-Love Slavery Picture of the Season, *Catch Me Some Freedom* became the Must-See, Must-*Hate* Event of the Year!

David

. . . Could that happen?

Kate

Let's say we ignore the Goldies! Sell it as something to shake a fist at! People love to hate-watch these days, David. And if it gets to be enough of a fire storm . . .

David

Idiots love to hate-watch, Kate.

Kate

Idiots are the only reliable demographic! Look at what's genuinely popular. *Hot Bods*! *Love Island*! *Gogglebox*! The news! They'll give anything their time!

David *thinks.*

Then he gets the phone back out and hits send.

David

Not when it comes to feature-length cinema. And not when it's about old sad brown people.

Kate

Is it though?! It's really about Chase Witley more than anything. And his hot bod, being very white and very sad about slavery for two hours.

David

That's a powerful message! They won't want to see that.

Kate

It isn't, at all, and that's exactly why they're gonna love it.

David

So what are you suggesting?

Kate

We don't hide *Catch Me Some Freedom* from the public, we make sure they can't *stop* hearing about it. That's our answer. The only way out, is in . . .

Her phone rings.

They both stare at the ringing phone for a few moments, considering it.

David

Kate, that's crazy.

Kate

I know but I'm out of ideas.

She answers the phone.

Kate (*to the phone*)
Hello?

David
Who?

Kate (*to* **David**)
Max!

Kate (*to the phone*)
Max! How are you?

David's *phone rings.*

David (*simultaneously, to the phone*)
David. Yeah. Yep. Yes. Yes, I meant it. I mean it. I'll –
yeah. Go ahead. Great.

Kate (*simultaneously, to the phone*)
No, Max, I'm not sure – right, yes of course. Let's talk right
after? Or? Sure. Okay.

David (*to the phone*)
Great.

They both hang up.

David *checks his email again.*

Kate
That was weird.

David
What?

Kate
Max was saying something about the film, but I had no
idea what he was talking about.

David (*unconvincingly*)
Weird.

Kate
Then he basically hung up on me. But, that's because the
ceremony's about to start. Let's get it up . . .

She finds a way to watch the ceremony.

Kate
I think we've done the best we – and again, as long as it
doesn't get too much attention here, we can pivot, David,
Smack Wave can *pivot*, I can see it all in my head. You'll
see. I am an un-campaign *queen*.

David
Kate, I have something to tell you.

Kate

What? It's starting, we should tune in.

David

Frank already told me what's going to be announced.

Kate

What? Wh – Frank Waverly?

David

Yeah.

Kate

He told *you*? What did he say?

David

Well –

Kate

David . . .

David

You recall, as Smack Wave Films, meaning principally the two of us, is involved /

Kate

/ Principally you –

David

But essentially us.

Kate

David, spit it out.

David

I shot Frank an email earlier. He understands the spot that I'm in.

Kate

We're in.

David

We're in, yes.

Kate

I know, that's why I –

David

So he understood, when I asked . . . to take my name off of *Catch Me*.

Kate

Take your . . .

David

But he said he had to keep yours. For the credits. For the nominations.

Kate

Mine? But it's a Smack Wave . . . film, and you're the head of –

David *holds up his phone.*

David

Not any more. I resigned about 90 seconds ago. Before the ceremony started.

Kate

David . . .

David

Want to know how *Catch Me* did?

Kate

David, are you saying –

David

It's the most nominated film in Goldie history.

Kate

No . . .

David

Yeah.

Kate

That makes us . . .

David

That makes *you* the most nominated producer in Goldie history. For Joe George Frampton's *Catch Me Some Freedom*.

Kate

David, I'll never live that down . . .

David

They needed a name, Kate. And I thought two would be too confusing. A scandal needs an epicenter, so . . . good luck.

Kate's *phone rings. She stares at it.*

David

I've been in this business a long time, Kate. You'll want to answer that. The press does not like to be kept waiting. And I'd say, with the whole Black Thing, you have a lot of explaining to do.

A second phone rings.

Kate *answers both phones, and puts one to her ear, then the other to her other. Speechless.*

She nods a few times.

Kate

Yes . . . Thank you . . . Well, Smack Wave was founded to tell stories, and we're all very proud of the film. We could not be happier for Chase. It's like a dream come true.

She meets **David**'s *eyes.*

David *flashes two thumbs up.*

David

I knew you could do it.

Blackout.

The End.

Black Bat
est. 2017

A Tasteful Addendum

<u>*CATCH ME SOME FREEDOM*</u>

a Joe George Frampton Experience

shepherded by

Joe George Frampton

Licensed by
SMACK WAVE FILMS

With the participation of
TURNER & TURNER GROUP

and
GREEN TURTLE PRODUCTIONS

MAMA GERTRUDE, a strong woman who has seen it all and then some, washes some pork chitlins for her family's supper.

She has an odd but trusting relationship with MASSA COLE (sic.), who gave her the Irish wristwatch on her left arm.

She cusses at DROWSY PHILIP and stands, perplexed.

> MAMA GERTRUDE
> Dang.

She moves towards the window of the wooden (<- *look this up*) shack. Peers out the whispy fields at the glowing, promiscuous moon, a voyeur on their private moment. As, in effect, are we, the spectator.

As she speaks her ancient wisdom into our lubricious ears, CHARLIE JOE sneaks in and sits, enraptured by her wisdom.

> MAMA GERTRUDE
> Philip I's scared. I reckon I ain't
> nevah been scared in all my
> Earth'ly life but I is now. You
> wan' know why, Phil? Jubah?
> Cleithandra? Bram? Lil' Gertrude?
> Hank? Father Omeethus? Lively
> Philip? Old Doc Hakapunye? Solomon?
> Junebug? Brian? Because I ain't
> nevah been this long without
> hearin' Massa Cole's voice in my's
> ear. And I ain't scared because he
> ain't here, now. I's scared because
> part of me wonders how he's doin'.
> And that's't done scared me, fam.
> There I go again. "Fam." What a
> term to use. I's been readin' the
> dictionary Miss Carruthers done got
> bought by her father-in-law two
> Christ-mass days ago. And I's right
> proud to say I learned'd every word
> off by heart. All of them.
> Disqualify. Germane. Turpitude.
> Inconsequential. Mordant.
> Voluminous. Ergonomic. Chitlins.
> There ain't's a word I don't
> consider myself at least somewhat
> partially famil'yer with. And
> that's why -

Overcome, CHARLIE JOE adds:

> CHARLIE JOE
> I believe, what Mama Gertrude is
> saying, family, is that now more
> than ever we need to be strong.
> What's more -

BRAM interrupts and stands, pruriently.

>   BRAM
>   Who's you callin' family, you white
>   boy?!

A ruckus.

FATHER OMEETHUS comes to CHARLIE JOE's rescue.

>   FATHER OMEETHUS
>   Let the boy SPEAK!

There is a clamor and commotion among the EMANCIPATED.

>   MAMA GERTRUDE
>   NO!

A hush falls.

MAMA GERTRUDE commands their attention.

>   MAMA GERTRUDE
>   He may well be, a white boy, Bram.
>   You's is right. You's is...
>   veracious.

There is general agreement and awe among the EMANCIPATED.

Someone starts singing.

>   MAMA GERTRUDE
>   But this here white boy...

She grips CHARLIE JOE's shoulder, caringly.

>   MAMA GERTRUDE
>   He's is alright.

They embrace.

CUT TO:
A MAJESTIC SOUTHERN RIVER.

CHARLIE JOE bathes thoughtfully, reflecting on his new life.

He catches the eye of an INNOCENT DEER, and nods
respectfully. He is now more cognizant of the circle of life.

                                        a SMACK WAVE FILM

CHARLIE JOE balks at the words BAILEY CARRUTHERS, the wizened
patriarch, just uttered.

> CHARLIE JOE
> In truth Mr. Carruthers, I cannot
> abide such a statement. This
> woman's a sweet and gentle
> creature, shrewd as a jackrabbit.
> If Bessie had meant you harm, she
> damned well would have done some.

JUNIOR CARRUTHERS balks at this.

> JUNIOR
> Damn you, Shimley. If we ain't
> never had let you on this
> damnnabbed plantation we's never
> had had to've been forced to be
> messed 'round with'n your
> cantankerous tinkerin' no how.

> MISTER CARRUTHERS
> Quiet, Junior. Mr. Shimley here
> might not know his place on this
> here plantation, but he and we know
> one thang's for certain. He's a
> white man, son, and you don't go
> cussin' no white man still wearin'
> his ridin' britches.

> CHARLIE JOE
> I ain't wearin' no britches. I's
> never believed in 'em.

> MISTER CARRUTHERS
> Oh?

> CHARLIE JOE
> Yeah.

> JUNIOR
> Oh?!

> CHARLIE JOE
> Yeah!

> BESSIE
> Oh mercy!

> CHARLIE JOE
> Look what you've gone and done,
> you've upset Bessie! You and your
> dangnabbed, rock-brained
> *intolerance!* What have you *got* up
> in there, *rocks* for *brains?!*

JUNIOR balks.